Oisin Murphy

OISIN MURPHY

BIOGRAPHY:

The Life And Career Of A Jockey Star

Dana Collier

Oisin Murphy

All rights reserved. No part of this publication may be reproduced, distributed, or transmitted in any form or by any means, including photocopying, recording, or other electronic or mechanical methods, without the prior written permission of the publisher, except in the case of brief quotations embodied in critical reviews and certain other non commercial uses permitted by copyright law.

Copyright © Dana Collier, 2024

Oisin Murphy

TABLE OF CONTENTS

INTRODUCTION

CHAPTER 1: MEET OISIN MURPHY
1.1 Early Life
1.2 Childhood In Killarney
1.3 First Encounter With Horses

CHAPTER 2: THE FIRST RIDE
2.1 Instruction At The Nearby Stables
2.2 Drawings From Legends Of Racing

CHAPTER 3: ENROLLING AT THE RACING ACADEMY
3.1 Early Contests
3.2 Overcoming Initial Difficulties

CHAPTER 4: BREAKING INTO THE BIG LEAGUES
4.1 First Career Victory
4.3 Important Early Races

CHAPTER 5: ASCENDING THE HIERARCHY
5.1 Significant Wins
5.2 The Strength Of Cooperation

CHAPTER 6: THE CHAMPION HANDICAPPER
6.1 Celebrations And Acknowledgments
6.2 Preserving The Elite Form

Oisin Murphy

CHAPTER 7: INTERNATIONAL COMPETITION
7.1 Cultural Encounters
7.2 Worldwide Acknowledgment

CHAPTER 8: INJURIES AND RECOVERY
8.1 Personal Struggles
8.2 Acknowledging Setbacks

CHAPTER 9: EXISTENCE OUTSIDE THE LINES
9.1 Hobbies And Personal Interests
9.2 Friends And Family

CHAPTER 10: MOTIVATING EXPERIENCES
10.1 Remarkable Events
10.2 Getting To Know Fans
10.3 Motivational Sayings

CHAPTER 11: GOALS FOR THE FUTURE
11.1 Broadening Perspectives
11.2 The Heritage
11.3 Influence

CHAPTER 12: WISE WORDS
12.1 Inspiration And Drive
12.2 Final Reflections

CONCLUSION

Oisin Murphy

INTRODUCTION

In the world of horse racing, few names resonate as profoundly as Oisin Murphy. A jockey who epitomizes passion, perseverance, and dedication, having traveled from the scenic environs of Killarney to the most opulent race tracks worldwide. This book explores the life of Oisin Murphy, a celebrity whose outstanding accomplishments and motivational tale have enthralled both admirers and would-be riders.

Oisin was raised with an intense curiosity and a natural skill, having grown up in a household that taught him to appreciate horses and the excitement of racing. It was evident he was destined for greatness from the minute he got on a pony for the first time. This book recounts his early years, emphasizing the critical events that molded his personality and stoked his desire. Oisin's path is a tribute to the strength of ambition and the unwavering pursuit of perfection, not simply racing.

Oisin Murphy

We will learn about Oisin's struggles both on and off the track as we examine his ascent to prominence in the cutthroat world of horse racing. His determination was put to the test by personal hardships, injuries, and the demands of fame, but each setback served as a springboard for improvement and self-discovery. The resilient narrative of Oisin demonstrates to us that possibilities for growth and learning may often be found along the way to success.

The life of Oisin off the track is clarified by this biography. His hobbies, social circles, and dedication to giving back to the community all point to a well-rounded person. Oisin epitomizes what it means to be a great sportsman—someone who recognizes that success is determined by more than just winning medals—but also by the influence he has on others around him. Beyond the realm of sports, his commitment to child mentoring, equestrian welfare, and mental health awareness is really remarkable.

Oisin Murphy

You will travel across countries and experience the exhilaration of competing on a worldwide scale as they read this book. Oisin's travels overseas not only display his skill but also the diverse range of experiences and cultures that have molded him into the person and competitor he is today. Oisin's worldwide racing career is a testament to a love that has no boundaries, taking him from the bright racetracks of Europe to the busy stadiums of Asia and beyond.

The purpose of this biography is to motivate the next rider and horse racing generation. Oisin's tale serves as a reminder that goals may be accomplished with diligence, fortitude, and a steadfast faith in oneself. With its insights into the attitude and strategies that might lead to success in the fiercely competitive world of horse racing, each chapter acts as a guide.

Get ready to be inspired by the life of rider Oisin Murphy as you read this book—a jockey who rides for more than just victory. The sport, the horses, and the unwavering spirit of those who dare to follow their

Oisin Murphy

ambitions are all celebrated throughout his trip. Come along as we explore the lives of a genuine racing star, whose tale is just getting started.

Oisin Murphy

CHAPTER 1: MEET OISIN MURPHY

A teenage rider whose path has captured the hearts of industry insiders and spectators alike is one of the brightest personalities in the colorful world of horse racing. His remarkable riding abilities and natural affinity for horses have made him a household figure in the industry. In a career already replete with awards and exhilarating triumphs, he personifies the spirit of passion and drive that characterizes a legendary champion.

He was destined for greatness from the moment he stepped foot in the racing world. In addition to catapulting him to the top of the sport, his personality and unwavering work ethic have served as an inspiration to many budding jockeys. Every race he participates in is more than simply a contest; it's a spectacle in which he displays his skill and in-depth knowledge of the animals he rides. Because of his ability to bond with his horses,

Oisin Murphy

he enjoys the respect of his colleagues and the affection of racing fans around the world.

More than simply a string of victories, his path serves as a reminder of the value of tenacity and the strength of aspirations. He keeps pushing the envelope and redefining what it means to be a successful jockey with each obstacle he encounters. Fans are excitedly awaiting the next chapter in his incredible journey, and as he moves forward, the enthusiasm around his future is evident.

1.1 Early Life

Irish jockey Oisin Murphy was born on September 6, 1995, into a family that valued the grace and excitement of horseback riding. His family's encouragement to follow his aspirations and their supportive atmosphere were crucial in helping him develop his interest. He was raised in a home that honored the relationship between horse and rider and where legends about historic races were often discussed over dinner.

His parents were involved in the racing world; they weren't simply spectators. They often brought him to neighborhood gatherings, where the noises and sights of the racecourse sparked his interest. He was driven to become a part of that world by the exhilarating spectacle of horses thundering down the stretch. This early experience showed him that racing was a vocation he was meant to follow, not just a pastime.

1.2 Childhood In Killarney

Raised in the breathtaking scenery of Killarney, his early years were filled with discovery and adventure. The stunning landscape, with its undulating hills and glistening lakes, provided an ideal playground for a little child who wanted to be a jockey. Killarney was more than simply a setting; it was a thriving community that promoted an appreciation of the outdoors, athletics, and, of course, horses.

He spent many hours outside in this beautiful location, frequently daydreaming about riding across the verdant fields. He found refuge in the neighborhood pony club, where he could hone his riding abilities and pick up new talents. He was surrounded by individuals who shared his enthusiasm, and, thanks to their encouragement, he flourished and soon distinguished himself from the rest of his class.

1.3 First Encounter With Horses

His life was changed forever by his first experience with a horse. In early childhood, he was introduced to a docile pony, his first horse. It was thrilling for him to get on the pony's back for the first time; he felt a surge of exhilaration and a sense of belonging that he had never known before. At that very moment, he realized he had discovered his genuine interest.

He became deeply appreciative of horses' power and beauty as he spent more time with them. Every ride was an experience that included learning, bonding with the horse, and plenty of laughing. He soon saw the value of trust and communication, understanding that a successful relationship requires a connection based on empathy and respect in addition to talent.

His confidence increased with each ride, and he started to focus on a career in racing. His developing aptitude was put to the test at the neighborhood pony club, where he seized every chance to hone his abilities. His

Oisin Murphy

commitment was clear, and the road ahead began to take shape as he evolved from a little child dreaming of racing to a determined rider.

Oisin Murphy

CHAPTER 2: THE FIRST RIDE

Everything changed the instant he flung his leg over the pony's back. The type of bright day that seemed to go on forever was here, full of promise for adventure. A surge of excitement swept over him as he found his seat. His delight was sensed by the delicate creature underneath him, and the two of them ventured into a realm that would soon become a lifetime obsession. It was a wonderful event that started a fire inside of him; that first ride was more than simply a physical encounter.

He could feel his own pulse synchronizing with the horse's motions with every leisurely trot. The rider-horse relationship became all that mattered as everything blurred around him. He felt as if the horse was nudging him to enjoy the pleasure of the ride by whispering secrets of joy and freedom. This first encounter laid the groundwork for a lifelong passion for riding that became stronger with time.

Oisin Murphy

The pony's stride changed from a timid walk to a lively canter as he acquired confidence. Laughter erupted from the pure delight of being at one with the horse. This was an awakening rather than just a hobby. It dawned on him that the bond he experienced was not only with the horse but also with the racing culture itself—a graceful, fast-paced dance based on trust.

Oisin Murphy

2.1 Instruction At The Nearby Stables

Now that he had experienced his first thrilling ride, he was excited to explore the world of horses further. The nearby stables became a haven for him to grow and learn, serving as his second home. He was surrounded by knowledgeable trainers here who understood his enthusiasm and were more than happy to help him along the way. They became mentors, giving him advice and assisting him in honing his abilities.

Training sessions were a time of laborious labor, humor, and teamwork. He discovered the value of giving the horses proper care and grooming, realizing that mutual respect and trust are the foundation of a solid relationship. Whether it was getting the hang of leaping or honing his riding stance, every day presented a new challenge. He was determined to learn all that was taught to him, and he approached every class with that in mind.

As experienced jockeys warmed up for races and novice riders warmed up, the stables were alive with activity. He

Oisin Murphy

was astonished as the more experienced riders showed off their abilities and glided the circuit with elegance. Motivated by their skills, he exerted more effort and resolved to forge his own path in this exciting realm. He discovered camaraderie, support, and a common love of horses at the stables, which served as more than simply a place to ride.

2.2 Drawings From Legends Of Racing

He became enthralled with the tales of the racing greats who had come before him while he trained. The stories of legendary riders who had overcome great obstacles fueled his aspirations and sparked his creativity. He studied movies, read a ton of books, and kept up with every race, learning the tactics and approaches that had made these athletes successful. Every narrative acted as a reminder that winning in horse racing required more than just skill—it also required tenacity, commitment, and an unwavering spirit.

He was especially fascinated by the tales of people who had overcome hardship and come out on top. Their stories struck a chord with him, showing that obstacles were often in the way of achievement. He discovered that obstacles were not signs of failure but rather opportunities for development and progress. This realization gave him courage and perseverance, inspiring him to follow his ambitions with unyielding commitment.

Oisin Murphy

He used to shut his eyes during the calm periods at the stables and picture himself riding with these legendary athletes, experiencing the surge of adrenaline as they raced to victory. This mental image developed into an effective tool that enabled him to see his future and the difference he wanted to make in the racing industry. He was driven to make his imprint on the sport and set high standards for himself after being inspired by their legacies.

Beyond their accomplishments, these racing icons had a profound impact on him; what really motivated him was their enthusiasm and love for the sport. He realized that racing was about more than just the prize—it was about the bond between the horse and the rider, the excitement of the race, and the satisfaction of having contributed to something greater. This realization strengthened his love for the game and fueled his ambition to become a jockey who upheld the traditions of the past while also reaching the pinnacles of performance.

Oisin Murphy

As he trained and rode more every day, his desire to become a professional jockey became brighter. A strong impetus was generated by his early experiences, the stables' encouragement, and the motivation he took from racing heroes. From a small child with a big dream to a determined rider, he was now ready to take on the journey of a lifetime with passion and dedication.

Oisin Murphy

CHAPTER 3: ENROLLING AT THE RACING ACADEMY

As his love of riding began to take off, it made sense to pursue it as a career. The famed Racing Academy, which is well-known for developing young talent and molding future sports stars, loomed large in the distance. He applied, knowing that this was his chance to advance further into the world of professional racing. He had an ambitious heart and a receptive mind.

As soon as he entered the institution, he sensed the electrifying atmosphere that was infused with ambition and resolve. He was surrounded by ambitious jockeys and experienced a culture that valued hard work and performance. The school provided a demanding curriculum that integrated academic knowledge about horse care, racing tactics, and the nuances of the sport with actual riding abilities. Here, he would learn riding skills as well as racing fundamentals.

Oisin Murphy

Lessons, practice sessions, and exercises took up early mornings and late evenings during the academy's rigorous training schedule. He was challenged intellectually and physically, yet he flourished in this setting. He welcomed every day's challenge because he knew it was the starting point for his future profession. Students' friendships fostered a sense of community as they laughed, struggled, and celebrated successes together.

The academy's professors were seasoned experts, each having overcome hardship and succeeded in their own unique way. They developed into mentors who helped him navigate the challenges of being a jockey and taught him the importance of self-control, resiliency, and respect for the horses. His desire was spurred by their encouragement and observations, and he was eager to make the most of this amazing chance, soaking up their expertise like a sponge.

Oisin Murphy

3.1 Early Contests

His training was going well, and soon he felt prepared to enter the world of professional racing. He was nervous and excited before the first race, which was obvious when he got on his horse. With the roar of applauding spectators and the distant thud of hooves on the track, the mood was intense. He was eager to show himself, as this was the chance he had been waiting for.

His first contests were emotional roller coasters. With every race came new difficulties, and he soon discovered that the plan was the only thing that equaled the excitement of competition. He researched the route, evaluated his rivals, and concentrated on developing a close bond with his horse. Their friendship grew vital as they realized that communication and trust were necessary for success on the track.

The early races were not without their challenges, although they were thrilling. There were experienced cyclists competing against him, and they all had different

Oisin Murphy

styles and strategies. Nevertheless, he entered every race with a determined mindset, seeing every failure as a teaching moment. His enthusiasm was further stoked by the rush of finishing, regardless of whether he was in first position. His goal was to get closer with each race.

During this period, the assistance he received from his other academy students was priceless. They encouraged one another, gave advice, and shared triumphs. This feeling of camaraderie strengthened the notion that they were all in this together and made the obstacles of competitiveness seem less overwhelming. Friendships forged in these early events would last a lifetime because of a mutual passion for the sport.

3.2 Overcoming Initial Difficulties

It soon became clear that navigating the world of professional racing was not without its difficulties. There was a lot of competitiveness and pressure to perform. There were times when he wondered whether he had what it required to succeed, and self-doubt seeped in. But it was in these uncertain times that he found his real power.

Learning to handle the highs and lows of racing was one of the biggest obstacles he had to overcome. While the rush of winning was incredible, losing might have a depressing effect. He learned how to accept both, realizing that each event helped him develop as a rider. The secret was to stay committed to his objectives and turn setbacks into opportunities for growth. This was a life-changing mental adjustment that made it possible for him to see impediments as possibilities rather than barriers.

Physical difficulties also surfaced. Peak physical condition was necessary for the demands of racing, so he committed to an intense training schedule. It became routine to spend the early mornings jogging, doing weight training, and perfecting his riding techniques. Learning about nutrition, hydration, and recuperation helped him realize that taking care of his body was just as important as learning how to ride.

Having his family and mentors there for him during difficult times was crucial. Even in difficult times, he was motivated to keep moving forward by their unwavering faith in his potential. They served as a reminder of his enthusiasm and initial motivations for his trip. His commitment to his ambition and ability to overcome hurdles were fueled by this support, which turned into a source of strength.

He gained a stronger comprehension of the nuances of the sport as he advanced through the academy and into the early contests. He gained the ability to assess racing circumstances, adjust to various courses, and interpret his horse's and his rivals' actions. He was able to acquire an advantage by using this analytical approach, which allowed him to make tactical choices during races that helped him stand out from the competition. Every race turned into a master class in flexibility and resiliency, imparting knowledge that would benefit him greatly in the future.

He was able to weather the usual ups and downs of racing because of the friendship he had with his fellow riders. They fostered an atmosphere in which vulnerability was greeted with sympathy rather than condemnation by sharing tales of their own setbacks and victories. His determination was strengthened by this fraternity, which served as a constant reminder that all athletes endure difficulties; what really distinguishes a champion is how they overcome those difficulties.

Oisin started to make a name for himself in the racing world with pure willpower. His skill and hard work paid off, and he began to get acclaim in regional tournaments. After years of training, dreaming, and tenacity, the exhilaration of winning his first race was beyond words. An instant that gave meaning to his sacrifices and inspired him to do more.

Oisin came to the realization that the voyage was just as significant as the goal as he proceeded down his route. Every competition, every difficulty, and every moment of uncertainty were woven together to form his career. He discovered that a person's love and devotion to a sport are more important indicators of success than mere medals or honors. He developed personally and as a rider with each race, becoming more prepared to go on the next exciting phase of his incredible trip.

Oisin Murphy persevered through hardship and came out stronger, more motivated, and more focused than before. Although achieving professional racing presented many obstacles, it also offered many chances for development and self-discovery. He was ready to take the racing world by storm because of his unwavering energy and ambitious heart. He was also eager to follow his ambitions and motivate others along the way. The best was still to come, and the voyage had only just started.

CHAPTER 4: BREAKING INTO THE BIG LEAGUES

The journey from aspiring jockey to professional competitor is an exhilarating and intimidating one, characterized by the terror of expectations and the promise of dreams coming true. For Oisin Murphy, it was an exciting and nerve-wracking occasion. He was eager to make a name for himself in the broad and competitive racing world, despite its many experienced competitors. He accepted the risk, eager to meet the difficulties that lay ahead, his heart full of ambition.

Years of commitment and sacrifice culminated in Oisin's first professional race. The track had an electrifying atmosphere, permeated by the aroma of freshly cut hay and the sound of hooves striking the ground. An adrenaline rush shot through his veins as he got on his thoroughbred, a blazing thoroughbred. He was prepared to make this dream come true because it was the moment he had been dreaming of for so long.

Oisin Murphy

As the starting gates flew open, a burst of energy shot through Oisin. His attention was drawn to the race's rhythm and the background noise produced by the spectators. He transformed every bend and straightaway into a canvas on which to paint his approach. He followed his instincts and worked his way through the group to set himself up for the decisive fight. He was racing not only against other people in those breath-taking seconds but also against himself, testing the boundaries of what he thought he was capable of.

It was a weird feeling to cross the finish line first, with a cacophony of acclaim and shouts echoing in his ears. Oisin was in disbelief—he had succeeded! The win validated all of the early mornings and late nights spent practicing; it was more than just a personal success. His future aspirations would be fueled by the waves of euphoria that came over him upon realizing he was now a professional jockey.

Oisin Murphy

The horse racing world was now watching Oisin Murphy as he made his formal entry into the big leagues with his first victory. After embarking on this voyage, he was ready for all the amazing challenges and experiences ahead.

4.1 First Career Victory

It was more than simply a race for Oisin to earn his first professional victory; it was a turning point that would mold his identity as a rider. He had a thrilling mixture of fear and excitement as he got ready for the occasion. Even though the pressure and stakes were high, he knew he was prepared. He was prepared to face the exhilaration of competition head-on, because it was so seductive.

Oisin sensed an electrifying connection with his horse as the race got underway. They danced down the track together, their shared desire vibrating with every step they took. The finish line ahead was all that mattered, as the world around him became blurry. He recalled the many hours he had spent in the stables, the dirt and perspiration that had brought him to this point. All of the difficulties and setbacks he had experienced had prepared him for this.

Oisin Murphy

Oisin's pulse raced as they got closer to the finish line. He heard the applause from the audience, a chorus of support that helped him go ahead. He gave his horse a spurt of energy, telling it to give it all they had left. As the finish line approached, they gave it their all and crossed it to a jubilant cheer from the spectators. He'd done it! The sheer excitement was immense! He emerged victorious.

At that moment, something spectacular began. Oisin's first professional victory sent a message to the racing community that he was a serious contender in addition to being a personal accomplishment. It created fresh avenues for growth and recognition for this young rider with unquestionable skill and a strong will. He was becoming a brand, a representation of aspiration and optimism, and he was no longer simply a name.

In the days that followed, Oisin revealed his victory. Salutations were sent to him from family, friends, and even racing legends. Every message was a reminder of the encouragement that had propelled him forward. With

Oisin Murphy

his first victory, he had not only fulfilled a personal ambition but also encouraged others to follow their aspirations by demonstrating that everything is achievable with diligence and hard work.

4.2 Building Credibility

After recording his first win, Oisin Murphy started to build a reputation that would soon spread across the racing world. His skill became well recognized, and he soon gained notoriety as a rising star. Oisin stands out from the crowd in the close-knit racing fraternity because of his distinctive riding style and unwavering dedication. He was a breath of new air, a tornado of enthusiasm and fire, not just another jockey.

Oisin's confidence increased as he participated in more races. Learning to read race dynamics helped him understand performance-changing subtleties. He became adept at timing, learning when to exert pressure on his horse and when to back off. This calculated technique turned into his signature, winning him the admiration of fans, other riders, and trainers alike. Every race served as a chance for him to hone his abilities and demonstrate his increasing expertise.

Oisin Murphy

Oisin had a special bond with his horses, which added to his already excellent reputation. Because of his natural ability to read their moods, he was able to establish a relationship with them that went beyond simple riding. He guided his horses with soft nudges and encouraging remarks, clearly demonstrating his relationship with them. Because of their collaboration, he was a powerful competitor who could get the most out of his horses when it counted most.

As he gained victories, Oisin found himself in the limelight more often. The media took notice and began interviewing and writing about him. He was becoming a celebrity and a source of inspiration for young riders worldwide, transcending his status as just a name on a race card. Oisin welcomed his sudden fame and used it as a means of inspiring others and sharing his story. In his speech, he emphasized the value of perseverance, hard work, and enthusiasm and urged future riders to pursue their goals with the same zeal that he did.

Oisin Murphy

Growing notoriety brought with it more strain. Oisin had to walk the tightrope between ambition and worry as expectations grew. He discovered how to turn the pressure into drive by telling himself that each race was a chance for personal development. With this attitude, he was able to turn potential tension into motivation and push himself to new limits. He had a strong support system around him, including mentors and family, who kept him grounded and focused on the things that were really important.

As he entered more difficult races and often faced off against some of the top riders in the business, Oisin's reputation grew. Every triumph served as a stepping stone, demonstrating his diligence and hard work. His ambition to win was further stoked by the realization that he was now competing for others who believed in him rather than just himself.

Oisin Murphy

4.3 Important Early Races

As Oisin Murphy's career progressed, a few significant races emerged as turning points in his early career. Every race was more than simply a contest; it was a turning point in his life, complete with lessons learned, difficulties faced, and victories. Each of these races added to his burgeoning legend and helped mold him into the skilled rider he was becoming.

The esteemed "Royal Ascot" was one of the most iconic early races. For Oisin, this event—which is renowned for its illustrious past and competitive edge—was a dream come true. The smell of new grass and the rush of expectation created an electrifying environment. He felt the weight of expectations as he saddled up—expectations from all those who had encouraged him along the journey, as well as his own. This was his opportunity to shine on a major platform.

Oisin displayed his own riding style from the time the gates opened. He successfully completed the difficult course while showcasing both talent and planning. He felt a rush of adrenaline as they got closer to the finish line, and he gave his horse every ounce of energy he had. It was an enormous accomplishment to cross the finish line first, and it cemented his standing as a competitive racer. He will always treasure that moment as proof that dreams are absolutely capable of coming true.

The "Derby," a legendary competition, is a notable race that has produced many champions. It was a rite of passage to compete here, and Oisin understood how important this race would be to his legacy. He did well under pressure, even though the stakes were higher and the competition was fiercer. The race played out like a practice run, with every horse and rider striving for victory. Oisin moved through the pack with such skill and purpose that it was evident, his pulse thumping in time with the sound of hooves underneath him.

His mental toughness was put to the test in addition to his physical prowess throughout the Derby. He was overcome with a feeling of success as soon as he crossed the finish line. It was a race that would live in his memory, a reminder of his dedication to training and his unwavering quest for greatness. In these early races, every victory served as more than simply a triumph; each one opened doors to bigger chances.

These important races were more than simply contests; they were turning points that molded Oisin's personality and professional path. He gained invaluable knowledge about perseverance, tenacity, and the value of collaboration with every triumph. He realized that the connections he cultivated along the road and the principles he maintained were more important indicators of success than just victories. These early encounters set the stage for a career that encouraged numerous others to pursue their aspirations in the horse racing industry.

Oisin Murphy

CHAPTER 5: ASCENDING THE HIERARCHY

The rise of Oisin Murphy in the horse racing industry is an inspiring story of success, tenacity, and striving for greatness. Every victory he gained was not only evidence of his prowess as a jockey, but also of his steadfast spirit and the aspirations of those who stood by him. Oisin discovered that achieving success in racing was a path full of chances and obstacles, each of which helped to mold him into the champion he would eventually become.

Oisin was committed to leaving his imprint as soon as he entered the professional ranks. In his early races, he experienced both joy and fear, but he welcomed every obstacle because he understood that each race was an opportunity for improvement. Oisin developed confidence with each start and swiftly established himself as a rider with a special flare and an instinctive grasp of his horses. He would need this relationship if he was going to succeed.

Season after season, Oisin's triumphs piled up, each one more momentous than the previous. He immediately established himself as a recognizable figure in the winner's circle, praised for both his skill and charm and sportsmanship. His contagious zeal attracted both fans and competitors, solidifying his status as a revered character in the racing world. Oisin's quest was about encouraging people to follow their aspirations, just as he did, rather than merely focusing on his own accomplishments.

As he advanced through the ranks, Oisin realized that perseverance and hard work were the keys to success. He gained the ability to handle the strain that comes with competing in high-stakes events as each race presented new obstacles. Although the taste of success was delicious, his character was really fashioned by the lessons he learned from failure. Oisin's perseverance in overcoming difficulties became a defining characteristic of his work, encouraging people to see obstacles as chances for personal development.

More than simply winning races, his quest was about the relationships he made and the impact he wanted to leave behind. In addition to competing for himself, he was racing for the aspirations of innumerable others who had faith in him. He carried their dreams and goals with him to every victory, reminding himself that achievement was a common experience that could encourage and elevate others around him.

Oisin Murphy

5.1 Significant Wins

A thrilling series of triumphs that have irrevocably changed the racing world have dotted Oisin Murphy's career. Every significant victory was a turning point for the sport as a whole, as well as for him. His performance in the "Qatar Prix de l'Arc de Triomphe," which many see as the ultimate horse race, stands out among his accomplishments. There was a tangible sense of excitement building up to this occasion as Oisin got ready to take on the world's top jockeys.

The grandstands were packed with people on race day, and there was a palpable sense of excitement in the air. Feeling a rush of exhilaration, Oisin got on his horse and gazed out across the course. As soon as the race started, he settled into a rhythm and used a combination of cunning and instinct to steer his horse. A wave of resolve passed through Oisin as they got closer to the finish line. With one more push, he propelled his horse forward, and they were the first to cross the finish line. The thunderous applause from the audience signaled to Oisin that he had accomplished something really remarkable.

A crucial triumph also occurred in the storied and prestigious "Epsom Derby." Oisin was aware that this was an opportunity to display his skill on a large platform, thus the stakes were high. The jockeys were all focused and motivated, and the tension was evident as the horses were in order. As the starting bell sounded, Oisin's pulse raced. He soon regained his composure and placed himself strategically throughout the race.

Oisin took the initiative as they neared the last bend, weaving across a densely packed field with skill. He rode his horse as hard as he could, knowing that the finish line was in sight. It was an exuberant moment to cross the finish line first, confirming Oisin's position among the sport's growing talents. Not only was his triumph at Epsom a personal accomplishment, but it also served as a catalyst for young riders worldwide to pursue their dreams.

Oisin Murphy

Oisin's triumphs extended beyond these two esteemed events. He kept winning on a variety of circuits, exhibiting his distinct riding technique and strong bond with his horses in every one. He stood out from his colleagues because of his quick decision-making and ability to read a race. His talent and dedication impressed fans and jockeys.

Along with increasing his collection of awards, Oisin's victories served as an inspiration to other jockeys who aspired to be like him. He often thought about the value of tenacity and hard work, emphasizing to others that achieving success is a journey with ups and downs. perseverance, as well as the backing of a community that had faith in him. Every victory was a springboard, encouraging others to follow their aspirations and taking him one step closer to his goals.

5.2 The Strength Of Cooperation

Over the course of his career, Oisin learned that being successful in horse racing required more than just one person. Every outstanding jockey has a committed staff that helps them succeed. Oisin forged close relationships with grooms, owners, and trainers—all of whom were vital to his success.

He recognized that the preparation and condition of the horse had a significant impact on the jockey's performance. Oisin always tried to be open and honest with trainers about the horses he rode, offering advice and observations that would help them perform to the best of their abilities. As a result of this cooperative attitude, the team felt more united, creating an atmosphere where everyone was pursuing the same goal.

He understood the value of the grooms who cared for the horses. He tried to be approachable and thanked them for their diligence and hard work. This respect for each other as a team not only fostered friendship, but also improved

Oisin Murphy

the horses' overall performance. Oisin was always quick to give thanks to his colleagues for their contributions, understanding that their success was a result of their combined efforts.

5.3 Mentoring And Counseling

Over his career, Oisin's growth as a rider was greatly aided by mentoring. He was lucky to have a number of mentors who saw his potential and were eager to provide advice. He was able to refine his abilities and make sense of the intricacies of the racing industry thanks to the expertise that these seasoned riders and trainers imparted.

He was greatly influenced by a retired jockey who had been through the highs and lows of the industry. Oisin was taken under the mentor's wing and received priceless guidance on a variety of topics, including racing tactics and handling competitive pressure. They often discussed the psychological elements of racing, stressing the need for resilience and concentration. Oisin discovered that mental toughness was just as important to success as physical prowess.

He was motivated by the tales of other accomplished cyclists. He studied their professional lives, delving into their experiences and obstacles. His resolve was

Oisin Murphy

strengthened by this study, which also gave him a path forward for his own goals. He discovered that barriers needed to be overcome with tenacity and that failures were a normal part of the process.

Oisin made it a point to give back to the community that had helped him along the way as he rose through the ranks. He turned into a mentor himself, imparting to prospective jockeys what he had learned. Oisin was dedicated to assisting others in realizing their aspirations and recognized the value of mentoring in developing the next generation of riders. His path was about more than simply winning; it was about inspiring everyone around him and creating a feeling of camaraderie inside the sport.

CHAPTER 6: THE CHAMPION HANDICAPPER

The story of Oisin Murphy's rise to prominence as a rider is one of perseverance, talent, and an unwavering love for horse racing. As he rose through the ranks, each race served as a springboard for achieving the ultimate objective: becoming the much-sought-after champion rider. The season was tough, full of high-stakes races that tested his resolve as a rider and his mental toughness. Oisin was aware that he would need to continuously provide his finest work to defeat some of the world's top jockeys in order to win the championship.

The season's last stretch proved to be the pivotal point. Oisin rode with an intensity that enthralled critics and fans alike, bearing the weight of expectations on his shoulders. Every race was a fight, and his bond with the horses was evident as he made his way around the courses. He was able to elicit the greatest performances from his mounts because of his distinct approach, which

Oisin Murphy

was defined by an instinctive grasp of them. This combination produced a string of spectacular victories that culminated in the opportunity he had been striving for.

There was a tangible sense of excitement in the air as the final winner count was revealed. Not only had Oisin won the championship, but he had done it with an impressive lead. The overpowering feeling of accomplishment was a result of his uncountable training hours, commitment, and the team's and family's support. This triumph not only represented a major turning point in the athlete's career but also in the annals of horse racing history.

Oisin was ecstatic on the day he was formally declared champion jockey. The racing world gathered to honor him and acknowledge the perseverance and hard work that had led him to this peak. With a sense of pride, Oisin raised the trophy in the air, signifying his commitment and enthusiasm. It was more than simply a championship; it was about the experience that had made him into the rider he is today—the trials and victories along the way.

Thinking back on his win, Oisin realized that this was just the beginning. The title of champion jockey came with a tremendous deal of expectation and duty. He was now regarded as an inspiration to young riders and racing fans worldwide. He was motivated to leave a lasting impression on the sport he loved with this championship.

Oisin Murphy

6.1 Celebrations And Acknowledgments

For Oisin, winning the title of champion jockey was more than simply a personal triumph; it was a cause for celebration for all those who had helped him along the road. He received a ton of praise from the racing world, and the festivities that followed were amazing. Oisin was always the life of the party, enjoying the limelight that his accomplishments brought.

The racing world's elite were present at the lavish awards event. The cheers were loud when Oisin approached to accept his prize. He was proud of his family, who had supported him through good and bad times, as well as himself at that moment. His parents, who had fostered his passion for horses since he was a little child, glowed with pleasure as they saw their son realize his aspirations.

Oisin was besieged with interviews and appearances in the media in the days that followed. Using this chance,

Oisin Murphy

he spoke about his path and emphasized the value of persistence, hard work, and his team's everlasting support. He was honored not just for his skill but also for his modesty and commitment to the game. Oisin gained popularity fast and was respected for both his grace outside of the racetrack and his abilities on it.

The joy on social media was palpable as fans and other jockeys applauded him. Oisin spent time interacting with his fans and giving them behind-the-scenes looks at his life as a world-class jockey. His genuineness struck a chord with many, encouraging a new generation of horse racing enthusiasts to follow their dreams. The festivities honored the thriving sport's community as a whole rather than focusing just on him.

Oisin stayed grounded when the festivities came to an end. He was aware that enormous responsibility accompanied tremendous recognition. He was committed to using his position to support the sport he loved by speaking out in favor of aspiring riders and the significance of mental health in the racing industry. It

Oisin Murphy

was just the start of a fresh chapter full of chances to encourage and empower others; his journey was far from over.

6.2 Preserving The Elite Form

A successful jockey's life is about more than simply winning races; it's about being in peak condition and never settling for less than the best. Oisin knew that the true test was still to come after winning the title of champion jockey. He felt a great deal of pressure to do well every time, since the competition was so intense. He was aware that he needed to develop his abilities and push himself in order to remain at the top.

Oisin developed an intense training schedule that prioritized his physical and mental toughness in addition to his riding skills. Oisin's habit of working out first thing in the morning included strength training, cardiovascular, and flexibility exercises to make sure he was at his best. He was obviously committed to being in shape, knowing that improved performance on the racetrack came from having a stronger physique. He often gave prospective jockeys training advice, stressing the need for physical preparation in a sport where every second matters.

Oisin Murphy

Maintaining his peak form also required a tremendous deal of mental preparation. Oisin used mindfulness and visualization practices to improve his concentration during competitions. Being at the top put pressure on him, but he learned to deal with it and turned any anxiety into constructive energy. Even under the most trying circumstances, he was able to maintain his composure because of his mental toughness. He frequently discussed the importance of mental health in sports and promoted candid conversations about the challenges faced by athletes.

In an effort to grow, Oisin also examined his races to pinpoint areas in which he could have done better. He'd watch videos of his rides and analyze his style and thought processes. His dedication to ongoing development distinguished him from his rivals and demonstrated his ambition to not only succeed but also to become the finest version of himself. He often discussed the value of humility and the idea that no matter how successful one becomes, one can always improve.

Creating a solid support system was another essential component of keeping him in shape. Oisin assembled a group of experts around him, including sports psychologists, nutritionists, and trainers. Their knowledge provided him with insightful information that improved his tactics, both on and off the track. Additionally, he promoted partnerships among jockeys, exchanging insights and advice that bolstered a supportive and cooperative racing culture.

Oisin kept setting himself new objectives as the seasons passed. In addition to defending his championship, his goals were to set new benchmarks and smash records. His unwavering quest for perfection served as an example for everyone around him, demonstrating that success involves more than simply reaching the top—it also involves the effort and commitment needed to remain there. Oisin's tale served as a ray of hope for a lot of people, showing that everything is achievable with perseverance, hard work, and a passion for the sport.

CHAPTER 7: INTERNATIONAL COMPETITION

Opportunities for Oisin Murphy to compete internationally started to arise as his career developed. His adventure took on a new meaning when he experienced the excitement of competing abroad. The colorful racetracks of France hosted his first major international competition, when he competed in major races like the Prix de l'Arc de Triomphe. Fans from all over the world had gathered to see the best in the sport, and there was an electrifying atmosphere. Expectations weighed heavily on Oisin, but he relished the task and rode with a combination of eagerness and resolve.

Oisin was also exposed to a range of racing tactics and styles when traveling overseas. Every nation has a different strategy for horse racing, ranging from the intense training schedules in England to the extravagant festivities in Dubai. Oisin learned from local jockeys and trainers and accepted these differences. One of his best

Oisin Murphy

qualities was his ability to adapt; he was able to take the best aspects of many racing cultures and incorporate them into his own unique style.

His travels also brought him to famous races, such as Australia's Melbourne Cup and the United States' Kentucky Derby. Every race was a fresh experience with unique chances and difficulties. Oisin's ability to maneuver through these diverse settings demonstrated his adaptability as a rider and cemented his status as a top contender worldwide.

Oisin Murphy

7.1 Cultural Encounters

Racing overseas was a rich cultural experience in addition to a competitive one. In every nation he traveled, Oisin thoroughly immersed himself in the local ways of life and traditions. From enjoying regional food to taking part in celebrations, he realized that every race was a chance to establish a connection with the local people and culture.

He enjoyed nothing more in France than to savor Paris' cuisine, frequently dining with other riders and trainers. He had witnessed the vibrant atmosphere of the Melbourne Cup in Australia as racing and fashion came together to create a magnificent show. These cross-cultural interactions not only increased his knowledge but also helped him make international friendships.

Oisin would often consider how these events had influenced him as a person and as a jockey. Through the lessons learned from many cultures, one developed a sense of humility and respect for the global character of sport. He transformed into a racing ambassador by sharing his experiences and enticing people to appreciate the uniqueness of the equestrian community.

Oisin Murphy

7.2 Worldwide Acknowledgment

As his career as an international racer progressed, Oisin gained worldwide notoriety. Both media sources and race fans started to notice his accomplishments. He was praised as one of the sport's emerging stars and featured in media throughout the globe. With his newfound prominence came a feeling of duty since he was now looked up to by jockeys all around the globe.

Along with increasing his reputation, Oisin's success in international races created opportunities for collaboration and sponsorships. A lot of big names wanted to be associated with him because of his impact on the racing scene. He took advantage of these chances and used his position to promote the sport and encourage others to follow their dreams.

As Oisin reached important milestones, such as winning important international championships, the praise kept coming in. Though his victories were evidence of his perseverance and hard work, he never lost perspective, crediting his family, trainers, and the horses he rode for their support. He realized that although individual skill was vital, the racing community's collective effort was just as significant.

Throughout it all, Oisin never lost sight of his heritage, often traveling back to Ireland to support the sport that helped develop his skill. He shared his story with aspiring jockeys and inspired them to follow their own goals by participating in mentoring programs and charitable activities. As a successful jockey and an advocate for the sport, Oisin's legacy started to take form, encouraging the next generation of riders to aim high.

CHAPTER 8: INJURIES AND RECOVERY

Every rider in the fast-paced world of horse racing eventually suffers an injury, which is a terrible fact. Oisin Murphy was taken aback by his first serious injury. He was knocked from his horse during a particularly rough race; he landed awkwardly and broke his collarbone. Being ignored caused an even greater emotional toll than the physical suffering. He loved racing, and the idea of being away from the track was unsettling. Racing was more than simply his job.

The path to healing was difficult. Oisin found himself battling obstacles in his emotional and physical well-being. The physical treatment regimen and strength-building activities were part of the demanding recovery process. Nevertheless, he went into every workout determinedly, seeing himself back in the saddle. His dedication to getting well served as evidence of his character, demonstrating his fortitude and steadfast will.

Oisin Murphy

It was around this period that Oisin discovered the value of patience. Setting modest, attainable goals gave him comfort, as the hard grind of recuperating took the place of the exhilaration of racing. Every little accomplishment, like getting back to full range of motion or exercising without experiencing any discomfort, becomes its own milestone. He shared his experience on social media, offering advice and motivation to anyone who may be going through similar struggles. He used his failure as motivation.

Gradually making his way back to the track, Oisin found himself feeling appreciative of his beloved sport once again. Every race seemed to be a celebration and a sobering reminder of the effort it had taken to come back. His injuries not only made him more determined, but they also made him more sympathetic to other jockeys going through similar things. He became a safety champion for the sport, utilizing his position to spread the word about the value of appropriate gear, mental health, and training.

Oisin Murphy

Oisin's struggles throughout his recuperation made him a stronger competitor. Not only was he a better jockey after that encounter, but he also became a more sympathetic person who was ready to help others along their path. He overcame his obstacles by using them as stepping stones and moving on with a fresh sense of purpose and resolve.

8.1 Personal Struggles

Under the glamor and flash of being a celebrity jockey, Oisin had to deal with personal challenges that tested his patience. He often felt a tremendous deal of pressure to perform at his best. Self-doubt may arise from the pressure to perform well from sponsors, trainers, and fans. Oisin began to wonder whether he could live up to the expectations that his own achievements had placed on him.

Oisin found comfort in his friends and family during these trying times. He recognized the need for having a solid support network to fall back on in difficult times. He gained perspective by talking to loved ones, who also reminded him of the happiness that racing had brought into his life. They helped him regain his enthusiasm by encouraging him to focus more on the sport's enjoyment than the pressure of winning.

In order to deal with his personal issues, Oisin also resorted to mindfulness and mental health techniques. He came to understand the benefits of visualization and meditation, which enabled him to control his anxieties and stay focused. By making time for introspection, he gained the ability to embrace vulnerability and acknowledge that failures were an inevitable part of any path. He was able to address obstacles with more clarity and positivity because of his increased insight.

Though not always simple, the process of self-discovery was transformational. Oisin started to realize that tenacity and personal development, rather than just successes, are what really characterize genuine success. He started talking more honestly to fans and other players about his difficulties. By doing this, he created a feeling of community and inspired others to talk about their own struggles and look for help.

Oisin became stronger and more centered as a result of his personal problems. He discovered that it was important to honor both his victories and the lessons he had learned from hardship. His experience served as a potent reminder that facing one's issues head-on can result in significant personal development, and that vulnerability is not a sign of weakness but rather a strength.

Oisin Murphy

8.2 Acknowledging Setbacks

No matter how good or competent a rider is, losses are inevitable in the realm of professional racing. Oisin Murphy had his fair share of setbacks, but every one was a learning lesson. One of his most noteworthy losses occurred in a significant race in which he was favored to win. He tried his hardest, but he ended very short of the podium. Although Oisin could feel the sadness, he understood that every failure taught him something important.

Oisin changed his perspective to one of introspection rather than moping over the setback. He watched the race, examined the video, and evaluated his choices. What more may he have done? Were there any elements that he had overlooked? He was able to convert a difficult experience into a teaching moment by using an analytical approach to pinpoint areas that needed development. He was aware that every setback was an opportunity to improve his tactics and abilities, making him a more potent opponent going forward.

Oisin also discovered the value of having humility while facing failure. Rather than assigning blame or offering justifications, he accepted responsibility for his work. He earned the respect of his colleagues for this level of responsibility, which reaffirmed his commitment to ongoing development. He had to constantly remind himself that failures happen to even the best athletes, and that overcoming hardships is the foundation of resilience.

Oisin made it a point to talk to supporters and aspiring jockeys about his experiences after each loss. He would often stress that failure is a necessary part of the trip and exhort people to see their setbacks as stepping stones in the direction of achievement. His open talks about losing struck a chord with a lot of people, turning what would have been a depressing event into a source of motivation. He demonstrated that failures do not determine a person's value or potential by being transparent about his challenges and fostering a culture of resilience.

Oisin Murphy

Oisin's losses made him bond more strongly with his colleagues and other riders. Their connections were deepened by their shared experiences, which made them stronger friends. They shared victories and helped each other through setbacks, creating an environment where learning from mistakes was acceptable and encouraged. Oisin's path benefited greatly from this feeling of community, which served as a constant reminder that he was never alone in his problems.

Oisin was more focused and motivated after each failure. He turned his losses into inspiration, which fueled his desire to do better and succeed. This fortitude turned into a defining quality of his personality, motivating not just himself but also everyone in his vicinity. As Oisin progressed in the racing world, he realized that every setback was just another chapter in his greater tale of tenacity and victory and that the road to success is often littered with obstacles.

CHAPTER 9: EXISTENCE OUTSIDE THE LINES

Despite the excitement of racing, Oisin Murphy has developed a full personal life that encompasses his many interests and principles. His life as a professional jockey is certainly exciting. The responsibilities of training and competition may make a jockey's life very demanding, but Oisin has perfected the art of striking a balance between his work and personal obligations. He feels that leading a balanced life enables him to compete at his best in every race, which propels his success on the track.

Oisin's commitment to fitness is one of the most important components of his life off the track. He knows that a successful racing career depends on being in top physical shape. His workout routine, which combines aerobic, weight training, and flexibility exercises, is nothing short of amazing. Oisin encourages his fans to adopt fitness as a lifestyle by posting brief videos of his exercises on social media. He enjoys challenging himself and being active, whether it's at the gym or on a run.

Oisin's interests, however, go well beyond mere physical health. He is extremely passionate about music, which he uses to release his creativity and relax at the end of the day. Oisin often finds comfort in the melodies that speak to him while he is singing and strumming his guitar. Oisin likes to jam out with friends or just spend a peaceful evening listening to his favorite music, which has the power to unite people. It serves as a reminder that life is about more than simply racing—it's about appreciating the little things in life.

Travel is an important part of Oisin's life. His racing career has brought him to some of the world's most breathtaking places, from Tokyo's bustling streets to Ireland's verdant countryside. Oisin is excited about the chance to travel to new locations and interact with new people. Every trip provides a distinctive cultural experience. He enjoys sampling a wide variety of local cuisines, from gourmet dining to street food. His

Oisin Murphy

horizons are expanded by these travels, and they also fill his life with priceless experiences.

His views are centered on balance and self-discovery in life after the track. He firmly thinks that professional success is improved by achieving personal contentment. Oisin makes a meaningful existence for himself that keeps him energized and grounded by pursuing his hobbies, fostering connections, and traveling. His experience serves as a reminder that, while pursuing aspirations is essential, it's also crucial to take care of oneself.

Oisin Murphy

9.1 Hobbies And Personal Interests

Oisin Murphy is not a one-dimensional person when it comes to her own hobbies. His many interests, which mirror his lively personality, are woven into a tapestry of his life. He embraces fitness with the same enthusiasm as racing, making it one of his greatest pleasures. Oisin adheres to an intense training schedule that incorporates strength training and yoga because he feels that physical fitness is essential to his success as a jockey. In addition to keeping him in peak physical condition, his dedication to fitness provides him with a mental outlet that helps him maintain concentration and clarity in the middle of the craziness of competition.

He is a huge admirer of the arts, especially music. He enjoys playing the guitar, and he often lets the song run through him as he is relaxing and strumming. Friends call Oisin the "life of the party," and he often sings. He can express himself artistically via music, and it's a welcome diversion from the demands of his profession.

Oisin Murphy

On social media, he often discusses his musical journey and inspires others to pursue their own creative passions.

Oisin also enjoys reading a lot, often delving into works that motivate and excite him. He reads a variety of genres, from books that take him to new places to biographies of legendary sportsmen. Reading provides him with creative energy and insightful information that he can use in his personal and professional lives. Oisin reads frequently, despite his hectic schedule, because he believes that lifelong learning is critical for personal development.

Oisin's life is further enhanced by her desire for travel. Because of his racing career, he has had the opportunity to travel to beautiful places and experience many cultures. He loves the chance to travel to new places, sample the food, and make friends from a variety of backgrounds. Oisin encourages his fans to embrace adventure and see the world by frequently posting about his travels on social media. Every journey opens a new chapter in his life, replete with experiences and insights that mold his viewpoint.

Oisin's passion for life is evident in his hobbies and personal interests. He knows that pursuing these interests not only improves his health, but also contributes to his performance as a jockey. Beyond the racetrack, Oisin builds a peaceful existence by enjoying music, literature, exercise, and travel. His trip serves as a reminder that following one's passions is a necessary and not a luxury aspect of life.

9.2 Friends And Family

Oisin has a particular place in his heart for his family. He was nurtured in a close-knit family in Killarney, where he learned the importance of tenacity and hard work. His parents have always supported his profession by attending races and acknowledging his accomplishments. Oisin often gives his family credit for stabilizing him and acting as a solid support system, particularly during trying times.

For Oisin, friendship has similar significance. He has forged enduring relationships with other riders and trainers, fostering a spirit of friendship that transcends the racecourse. He may share the highs and lows of his job with these pals, who give him a feeling of support and belonging. Oisin treasures the relationships he has made within the racing community, whether it is by sharing a success or offering sympathy after a heartbreaking defeat.

Oisin Murphy

Aside from racing, Oisin also likes to hang out with his pals. He cherishes these times when he can unwind and refuel, whether it's going to the gym, seeing concerts, or just having dinner together. He is accessible due to his laid-back personality, and he often finds himself surrounded by a devoted group of friends that like life as much as he does.

9.3 Contributing To The Community

Oisin Murphy thinks it's important to return the favor to the community that has helped him along the way. He uses his position to raise awareness about a variety of issues by actively participating in philanthropic events and activities. Promoting mental health is one of his main priorities, as it's a subject that really speaks to him. Oisin has encouraged people to seek support and assistance when required by being transparent about the demands of racing and the value of mental health.

He participates in equine welfare groups and promotes humane treatment and upkeep of horses. He is dedicated to making sure that horses are handled with respect and compassion because he recognizes the special link that jockeys have with their rides. By sponsoring programs that advance horse care, Oisin shows his dedication to the sport and the creatures that make it possible.

In order to inspire the next generation of riders and fans, Oisin regularly participates in youth initiatives. In order to share his knowledge and perspectives with prospective jockeys, he often conducts seminars and mentoring sessions. His commitment to developing new talent is a reflection of his community values and the obligations that come with achievement.

CHAPTER 10: MOTIVATING EXPERIENCES

Oisin Murphy's horse racing career is not just a story of individual achievements; it is also enhanced by the fervent supporters who encourage him. Oisin's relationship with his followers has produced many moments of inspiration, whether at the busy racetracks of Ireland or the large stadiums of international racing. These encounters strengthen his resolve and serve as a constant reminder of the difference he makes in other people's lives.

During the 2019 Derby at Epsom Downs, there was a particularly unforgettable moment as Oisin crossed the finish line to the applause of a sea of supporters. His followers were beaming, and the atmosphere was electric. Oisin thinks about it a lot, how these times of shared enthusiasm improve his performance and foster a feeling of camaraderie among racing fans. Because jockeys and their supporters have a special link based on the same goals and aspirations, Oisin is inspired to give it his all each and every time he rides.

In 2021, Oisin had another inspiring encounter when he spent time with young fans who looked up to him as a role model at a charity event. It brought back memories of his own childhood dreams to hear about their dreams. It was a profound event that strengthened his resolve to make a positive impact on young people's lives by demonstrating to them that everything is possible with perseverance and hard work.

Oisin Murphy

10.1 Remarkable Events

During his career, Oisin has competed in races that his supporters will always remember. One such event was the Qatar Prix de l'Arc de Triomphe in 2020, which he won with a breathtaking ride. As the horses thundered down the last stretch, the tension was tangible, and Oisin's resolve was evident as he pushed his horse ahead. The rush of being the first person to cross the finish line was more than simply a personal accomplishment; it was a joint celebration with supporters who had put their faith in him.

Oisin had a difficult task in 2022 at the Royal Ascot, where there was a lot of competition. Even though he didn't win, his supporters were deeply affected by the manner in which he performed under duress and showed sportsmanship. They supported the notion that success is determined more by the heart and effort put into the race than by winning, admiring his tenacity and capacity to learn from every setback.

Oisin Murphy

Not only do these races mark significant turning points in Oisin's career, but they also forge enduring bonds with supporters who encourage him in times of adversity and celebrate his victories. Racegoers' tales about these events weave together a fabric of community that enhances horse racing and elevates it beyond mere competition.

10.2 Getting To Know Fans

Oisin Murphy knows how important it is to build relationships with his supporters, which is why he often makes time to see them at races, events, and charity activities. These exchanges are real moments of connection that Oisin treasures, not just required ones. Every fan, in his opinion, has a story to tell, and hearing them out helps him understand the variety of experiences and backgrounds that participants have that draw them to the game.

Fans flocked to Oisin's meet and greet session at the 2023 Cheltenham Festival, ready to express their enthusiasm and ask questions. With a contagious joy in the air, Oisin spent time interacting with everyone, exchanging giggles and signatures. This was a dream come true for a lot of admirers, and Oisin's friendliness and kindness made an ordinary meeting into a memorable one.

Furthermore, Oisin frequently updates his fans on social media about his jockey adventures. He makes it possible for followers to feel a part of his journey by providing them with intimate moments from his trips or behind-the-scenes looks at his training. Because of this openness, supporters come together with a shared love of racing and a sense of belonging.

Oisin Murphy

10.3 Motivational Sayings

Oisin Murphy has shared a lot of motivational sayings with his supporters throughout the course of his career. His mantra, "Success is not just about winning; it's about the journey and the lessons learned along the way," is one of his favorites. It expresses his conviction that every experience fosters personal development and encourages followers to embrace their own journeys, no matter how difficult they may be.

"Believe in yourself, even when the odds are against you," is another saying that has resonated with his admirers. Oisin's career has not been without difficulties, and his tenacity offers people hope when they are experiencing their own hardships. This statement reminds supporters that failures are only stepping stones to greatness and inspires them to keep going.

The phrase "Together, we can achieve greatness," which Oisin often uses to highlight the value of community, perfectly captures the essence of racing: spectators, riders, and trainers coming together around a common love. It encourages supporters to help one another, fostering a bond between them that goes beyond the racetrack.

CHAPTER 11: GOALS FOR THE FUTURE

Oisin Murphy's dreams of becoming a rider are as colorful as the silks he wears on race day as he looks to the future. He has laid out a plan for the next few years that displays his unwavering love for the game and his ambition to make a lasting impression. He has big goals for the future. His main goal is to win more renowned races around the world, including those that are well-known. Imagine the excitement of being the first person to cross the finish line at the Breeders' Cup or the Melbourne Cup; these events represent the height of success in horse racing and are not just about personal glory.

In the future, Oisin also sees himself as a significant figure in forming the next wave of jockeys. He is keen to impart his vast expertise to young riders, realizing that mentoring is essential to developing potential. He wants to encourage aspiring jockeys to embrace the virtues of tenacity, devotion, and sportsmanship by holding seminars and training camps. It excites him to think about sharing his expertise and enthusiasm, and Oisin believes he can improve his beloved sport by making future investments.

Oisin wants to increase the scope of his charitable work. His aim is to start a nonprofit that promotes equestrian care and mental health awareness. Through fund-raising and advocacy for these important issues, he hopes to establish a network of support for athletes and guarantee that horses get the attention and dignity they deserve. Oisin's dedication to giving back is a reflection of his principles and character, not merely a goal in and of itself.

He understands the value of ongoing learning and development. He intends to get fully immersed in every facet of the racing business, from horse management to training methods. He wants to increase his expertise in order to become a more knowledgeable jockey and supporter of the game. His work and contributions to the

Oisin Murphy

racing community will both be enhanced by this insatiable curiosity.

Oisin hopes that his experience will motivate and inspire others. He wants his narrative to inspire both admirers and aspiring athletes by demonstrating that everything is achievable with perseverance and hard work. Not only does he fight for the chance to win, but also for the chance to inspire others to follow their ambitions without fear.

Oisin Murphy

11.1 Broadening Perspectives

Oisin Murphy has goals that go far beyond the racetrack. He wants to experience new and exciting things and broaden his horizons. His main objective is to compete in races on international circuits that test his physical and mental limits. Imagine Oisin riding through Australia's beautiful landscapes or Hong Kong's bustling streets; these experiences would not only sharpen his talents but also introduce him to a variety of racing styles and cultures. Oisin is excited to take on the challenges that come with every new place.

The idea of breaking into the media and television world excites him. His innate charm and perceptive viewpoints might make him a compelling analyst or pundit who spreads his passion for the game to a wider audience. Imagine his contagious excitement pulling spectators along for the ride as he recounts the highs and lows of a race. This position can help Oisin demystify the sport and make it more approachable for beginners.

Oisin Murphy

Oisin is also eager to investigate joint ventures with companies that share his beliefs, especially those that emphasize animal care and sustainability. He is aware that the racing business is obligated to advance moral behavior, and he aspires to lead this effort. Oisin wants to fight for a better future for athletes and the horses they love by collaborating with groups who are committed to positive change.

Oisin also sees himself visiting new nations and being fully immersed in their customs. He thinks that these encounters will enlarge his viewpoint and improve his life in ways he is yet unable to fully comprehend. Oisin is keen to absorb information from his surroundings, whether it is via sampling regional specialties or participating in customary festivities. He will become a more likable and inspirational character with every journey that adds a new dimension to his tale.

His path is one of development and discovery. Knowing that every step he takes ahead will mold his character and profession, he strives to seize any chance that presents itself. He wants to show others that life is an adventure that is just waiting to be taken by pushing himself to the limit and pursuing new experiences.

11.2 The Heritage

Thinking back on his legacy, Oisin Murphy imagines a world characterized by compassion, excellence, and honesty. In addition to his accomplishments on the racetrack, he hopes to be recognized for the good he has done for the horse racing industry. Oisin hopes to leave a legacy that encourages the next jockey generations to follow their hobbies with purpose and uncompromising determination. He thinks that being able to inspire others while pursuing one's own goals is the key to ultimate success.

Oisin's conception of legacy includes his support for mental health and equestrian welfare. His goal is to develop initiatives that guarantee horses get the best care possible and highlight the importance of their welfare in the racing sector. Oisin hopes to make a lasting impact by supporting programs that advance humane care and retirement alternatives for these amazing creatures, honoring his passion for racehorses. His dedication to

Oisin Murphy

changing the game will inspire future riders to put the health of the horses they ride first.

Oisin wants his contribution to dismantling the stigma associated with mental health in athletics to go down in history. He intends to share his own experiences and inspire others to get treatment when necessary by using his platform to promote mental health. Oisin wants to provide a supportive atmosphere for athletes where vulnerability is seen as a strength rather than a weakness by encouraging an open discussion about mental health. This facet of his legacy has the potential to encourage players in other sports to give their mental health first priority, opening the door for a more sympathetic and understanding sporting community.

Oisin hopes to leave a legacy of mentoring by helping aspiring riders overcome obstacles in their professional lives. His goal is to establish a mentoring program that matches seasoned cyclists with novices to provide a sense of support and companionship. Oisin hopes to inspire the next generation of jockeys to handle the ups

Oisin Murphy

and downs of the sport with perseverance and confidence by sharing his path, observations, and lessons learned.

A scholarship fund for promising riders from disadvantaged backgrounds is another of Oisin's aspirations. He is aware that many gifted people may have difficulties accessing resources and training, and he wants to remove such obstacles. Oisin aims to ensure that skill and enthusiasm are the only requirements for success in the sport through opportunity and financial assistance. In addition to enhancing the racing community, his dedication to inclusion will encourage others to help the less fortunate and open doors for them.

His influence on the sport, the horses, and the people he meets along the journey will be remembered more than his accomplishments and records. He aspires to empower those around him and encourage others to follow their dreams by leading a life of integrity and purpose. His journey is proof of the strength of compassion, resiliency, and passion—strengths that will be felt long after he crosses the final finish line

Oisin Murphy

11.3 Influence

Oisin Murphy has more than just personal goals for the future; they also represent a larger desire to positively influence the world in which he lives. His objectives and projects will be well received by the racing public, up-and-coming riders, and fans alike. Oisin leads by example, pushing for significant causes and competing to the best of his abilities on the track.

His story serves as a reminder that one's ability to improve the lives of others is a more important indicator of success than awards and medals. Because of Oisin's dedication to advocacy and mentoring, the racing community will develop a supportive and empowering culture that will unite both spectators and riders.

Oisin epitomizes the spirit of resiliency and persistence as he pursues his aspirations. Many people find inspiration in his narrative, which shows that everything is achievable with perseverance, hard work, and a dedication to changing the world. His goals will have a lasting influence that encourages next generations to set lofty goals and pursue excellence, even beyond his own professional life.

CHAPTER 12: WISE WORDS

Oisin Murphy has a wealth of knowledge that he would be delighted to impart to all the ambitious young riders out there. He stresses the value of passion above everything else. "Work won't feel like work if you love what you do," he adds, citing his own experience. What propelled him to success was the excitement of competition, the camaraderie with horses, and the pleasure of racing. He exhorts aspiring riders to discover their passion, whether it is for horseback riding, horse care, or the exhilaration of a race. When things become hard, passion is the fuel that will keep you going.

Oisin also emphasizes the importance of perseverance and hard work. "In this sport, there are no shortcuts," he says. Success is the product of many hours of practice, education, and persistence; it does not happen suddenly. According to his advice, young jockeys should enjoy the grind, come early, and leave the stables last. Every ride, every lesson, and every race is a chance to improve.

Recall that all champions were once beginners who dared not give up.

Keeping an optimistic outlook is something else Oisin advises. A race's course may be unexpected, and obstacles will inevitably arise. "It's how you respond to those challenges that defines you," he observes. Instead of seeing challenges as barriers, he advises aspiring riders to see them as stepping stones. Positivity not only helps you overcome setbacks, but it also brings positive energy and opportunities into your life. If you surround yourself with positive vibes, you'll discover that even the most difficult days may result in amazing discoveries.

In the racing scene, networking is essential, and Oisin emphasizes the need for establishing connections with trainers, other riders, and business experts. "You never know who might open a door for you," he adds. He advises novice riders to be personable, to inquire, and to pick up tips from more seasoned riders. Every relationship you make has the potential to provide priceless possibilities and career-changing insights. So get out there, meet people, and create your own racing family!

Aspiring riders should never stop studying, he advises. There is always something new to learn in the ever-evolving racing business. "Avoid becoming bored," he says. Continuous learning will keep you ahead of the game, whether it's learning new equine care innovations, researching various riding styles, or comprehending horse behavior. Participate in seminars, study literature, and critically observe racing. Your chances of success will increase with your level of expertise.

12.1 Inspiration And Drive

Oisin wants the young people who dream of riding at the top levels to realize that their aspirations are real and doable. "Have faith in yourself," he exhorts. In a sport that often pushes your boundaries, confidence is essential. Oisin talks about his personal struggles with self-doubt, as well as how perseverance and self-belief helped him overcome them. "You're halfway there the moment you believe you can," he adds, urging aspiring jockeys to develop a strong sense of self-worth.

Oisin also stresses the importance of resilience. Like life, racing will always include disappointments. He tells us that "every great jockey has faced defeat." The secret is to grow from them and get back stronger every time. Young riders are urged by him to never give up, to learn from every setback, and to use it as fuel to go better. Recall that the route is a twisting one, with ups and downs, rather than a straight one.

Oisin Murphy

The group of other jockeys and horse enthusiasts is another source of inspiration. Oisin thinks that friendships may be quite uplifting. "He advises supporting one another, sharing in one another successes, and encouraging each other in trying times. The racing community, which is unique, may inspire you to set and achieve your goals. You two may motivate one another and build enduring relationships.

He also emphasizes how crucial goal-setting is. He says, "Short-term goals lead to long-term success." Setting attainable goals will help you stay motivated and focused, whether your goal is to get a local racing ride, improve your fitness, or perfect a certain skill. No matter how small the win, acknowledge it because it brings you one step closer to achieving your greatest goals. Recall that all champions began with a single aim!

Oisin encourages aspiring jockeys to enjoy the adventure. "Enjoy every moment, from the early mornings at the stable to the thrill of the race," he adds with a grin. The goal is not as significant as the trip.

Oisin Murphy

Treasure the relationships, the learning opportunities, and the passion for the game. Your performance will be joyful and inspirational to those around you when you are passionate about what you do.

12.2 Final Reflections

Oisin Murphy tells young, aspiring jockeys that every moment is a chance to develop and learn as he considers his path. "Take each day as it comes, and don't be afraid to make mistakes," he urges. Errors are not signs of failure but rather of progress toward achievement. Adopting this way of thinking can assist you in gaining flexibility and resilience, two qualities that are vital for any jockey. There are a lot of surprises in the racing industry; therefore, being willing to learn will make you stand out from the competition.

Oisin also exhorts aspiring riders to discover their own voice and flair in the sport. "Don't try to be someone you're not," he urges. Genuineness has immense power. Accept and value your unique qualities, whether they are related to your training methods, riding style, or relationship with your horses. Individuality is highly valued in the racing industry, and being true to yourself will improve your performance and draw in the correct possibilities.

He stresses how crucial it is to have a balanced life. "RACING is a huge part of who you are, but it's not everything," he adds. Mental and emotional health depend on making time for friends, family, and hobbies. Taking up interests outside of racing might give you a new outlook and help you rejuvenate. Whether it's participating in sports, discovering new music, or spending time in nature, find those activities that make you content and fulfilled.

Oisin wishes to encourage aspiring jockeys that life is about more than simply winning races; it's about the connections you make, the things you learn, and the person you grow into along the road. He exhorts, "Embrace every moment and don't forget to have fun." Your main priorities should always be the excitement of competition, the thrill of racing, and the pleasure of bonding with horses.

As you put on your riding boots and saddle, remember your role in a long history of fervor, commitment, and companionship. Every race offers a fresh experience and an opportunity to demonstrate your skill and passion for the game. The racing world is yours to rule if you have a dream-filled heart, perseverance, and a strong work ethic. Take to the world stage with passion and leave your mark!

CONCLUSION

It is clear as we draw to a close Oisin Murphy's incredible journey that it is about more than simply the victories and honors he has received. Resilience, passion, and an undying dedication to the sport and the community are all interwoven throughout the story. Oisin's story is a potent reminder that obstacles are a common part of the road to success, but what really makes us is how we overcome them.

Throughout this book, we've looked at Oisin's complex life. Every episode of his journey—from his modest upbringing in Killarney to his rise to prominence as a race car driver—has shown the commitment and diligence that have driven him to success. Oisin's path is proof that one can overcome challenges and accomplish greatness if they have a clear goal and a strong sense of determination.

Oisin is a man whose character shines through even outside of the racetrack, as we have seen with his dedication to charitable giving. His support of youth mentoring, equestrian welfare, and mental health emphasizes the value of utilizing one's position to further the common good. In addition to his racing accomplishments, Oisin exemplifies what it means to be a true champion by motivating others and improving society.

Let's not forget the lessons discovered along the route as we commemorate Oisin's accomplishments. Throughout his journey, themes of the need for balance in life, the importance of honesty, and the significance of perseverance in the face of hardship recur. These principles apply to anybody trying to follow their aspirations in any industry, not just aspiring jockeys.

Oisin Murphy is still on his road, and we can only imagine the amazing achievements he will accomplish as he leaves his imprint on the world of horse racing. Future generations might draw inspiration from his narrative, which shows that everything is achievable with perseverance and hard work. The racetrack serves

Oisin Murphy

as a venue for the birth, development, and realization of aspirations in addition to being a site for competition.

We hope that the spirit of Oisin's adventure stays with you after you shut this book. Whether you are a horse racing enthusiast, an aspiring jockey, or someone going through a difficult time in your life, I hope that his tale will encourage you to follow your hobbies and aspirations wholeheartedly. Keep in mind that every obstacle you face may be used to your advantage and that every race is a chance to improve.

We are grateful that you were able to go with us through Oisin Murphy's life. Your curiosity about his story suggests that you both have a love of the human spirit and a similar enthusiasm for the game. We really hope that you were encouraged by his victories and consoled by his hardships.

Have the courage to follow your passions, the fortitude to overcome obstacles, and the wisdom to give back to your community as you journey. The story of Oisin

Oisin Murphy

serves as a reminder that each of us has the ability to change people's lives as well as our own.

As you set out on your own journeys, both on and off the track, we encourage you to live up to Oisin's advice to "Ride with heart, embrace every moment, and always maintain your dream-filled belief. I hope you will always pursue your dreams and racing spirit. Thank you for reading.

Printed in Dunstable, United Kingdom